Boxer Dogs as Pets

The Complete Boxer Owner's Manual

Boxer Dogs Characteristics, Health, Diet, Breeding,
Types, Care and a whole lot more!

By Lolly Brown

Copyrights and Trademarks

Disclaimer and Legal Notice

Foreword

Developed in Germany, the Boxer is a short-haired breed dog whose coat is tight-fitting and what is considered a medium to big sized dog. Its smooth coat comes in the colors of fawn, white, brindle or not. Its broad shoulders make it stand proud amongst others. Its square muzzle and strong jaws not only makes it a handsome breed it is also designed to get a good grip on prey.

The Boxer is classified in the Working Group category of dogs and as you read further you will find out why this is so. You will also read more about why it is categorized under the Mossoler group of canines, which is a dog built solidly from a larger breed of dogs which all descend from the same ancestor, the Molossus, a large shepherd dog.

Your heart, reader, too has been captured by this elegantly funny canine - or you would not be reading this. The following sections have been compiled to give you a clearer understanding of what the Boxer is like, and hopefully help you come closer to understanding this fascinating canine whose utmost loyalty is one that is truthfully honest.

Table of Contents

Introduction

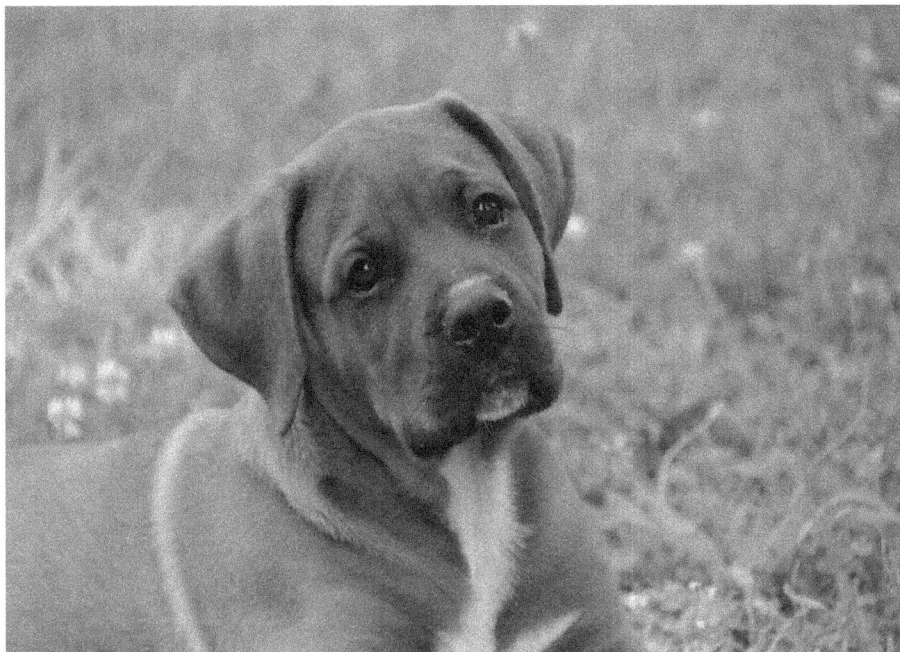

Many dog societies have come to recognize the truth in the honesty of the Boxer. It is lauded as one of the most fiercely loyal dogs to its guardians and is patient to children who show them respect. They are overall a loving bunch who lives on the nurturing love and companionship of the people it guards and vice versa. It is a playful sort who with positive reinforcement can be trained well in spite of its seeming stubbornness.

The Boxer is an amusing sort of canine with all the funny noises it emits. They hiccup, flatulent and burp just like you and I. Some even seem to understand guilt and embarrassment displaying what would seem like shame when called out after the deed.

They are unapologetic with regard to their playfulness and will not hold back when expressing their love and gratitude for their guardians and caregiver's attention. It won't be unusual for it to give a little shimmy and its signature kidney-bean dance when happy or excited. They are fiercely loyal pets and makes great companions during downtime and playtime.

Boxers of today are predominantly domesticated canines and have carved a niche as part of the working class and work side by side with their owners. They are still employed as the finest of many K-9 teams, flank their caregivers during hunting season and importantly assist many disabled patients. You will fall in love with the Boxers traits of loyalty, truthfulness and dependability.

Glossary of Dog Terms

AKC – American Kennel Club, the largest purebred dog registry in the United States

Almond Eye – Referring to an elongated eye shape rather than a rounded shape

Apple Head – A round-shaped skull

Balance – A show term referring to all of the parts of the dog, both moving and standing, which produce a harmonious image

Beard – Long, thick hair on the dog's underjaw

Best in Show – An award given to the only undefeated dog left standing at the end of judging

Bitch – A female dog

Bite – The position of the upper and lower teeth when the dog's jaws are closed; positions include level, undershot, scissors, or overshot

Blaze – A white stripe running down the center of the face between the eyes

Board – To house, feed, and care for a dog for a fee

Breed – A domestic race of dogs having a common gene pool and characterized appearance/function

Breed Standard – A published document describing the look, movement, and behavior of the perfect specimen of a particular breed

Buff – An off-white to gold coloring

Clip – A method of trimming the coat in some breeds

Coat – The hair covering of a dog; some breeds have two coats, and outer coat and undercoat; also known as a double coat. Examples of breeds with double coats include German Shepherd, Siberian Husky, Akita, etc.

Condition – The health of the dog as shown by its skin, coat, behavior, and general appearance

Crate – A container used to house and transport dogs; also called a cage or kennel

Crossbreed (Hybrid) – A dog having a sire and dam of two different breeds; cannot be registered with the AKC

Dam (bitch) – The female parent of a dog;

Dock – To shorten the tail of a dog by surgically removing the end part of the tail.

Double Coat – Having an outer weather-resistant coat and a soft, waterproof coat for warmth; see above.

Drop Ear – An ear in which the tip of the ear folds over and hangs down; not prick or erect

Entropion – A genetic disorder resulting in the upper or lower eyelid turning in

Fancier – A person who is especially interested in a particular breed or dog sport

Fawn – A red-yellow hue of brown

Feathering – A long fringe of hair on the ears, tail, legs, or body of a dog

Groom – To brush, trim, comb or otherwise make a dog's coat neat in appearance

Heel – To command a dog to stay close by its owner's side

Hip Dysplasia – A condition characterized by the abnormal formation of the hip joint

Inbreeding – The breeding of two closely related dogs of one breed

Kennel – A building or enclosure where dogs are kept

Litter – A group of puppies born at one time

Markings – A contrasting color or pattern on a dog's coat

Mask – Dark shading on the dog's foreface

Mate – To breed a dog and a bitch

Neuter – To castrate a male dog or spay a female dog

Pads – The tough, shock-absorbent skin on the bottom of a dog's foot

Parti-Color – A coloration of a dog's coat consisting of two or more definite, well-broken colors; one of the colors must be white

Pedigree – The written record of a dog's genealogy going back three generations or more

Pied – A coloration on a dog consisting of patches of white and another color

Prick Ear – Ear that is carried erect, usually pointed at the tip of the ear

Puppy – A dog under 12 months of age

Purebred – A dog whose sire and dam belong to the same breed and who are of unmixed descent

Saddle – Colored markings in the shape of a saddle over the back; colors may vary

Shedding – The natural process whereby old hair falls off the dog's body as it is replaced by new hair growth.

Sire – The male parent of a dog

Smooth Coat – Short hair that is close-lying

Spay – The surgery to remove a female dog's ovaries, rendering her incapable of breeding

Trim – To groom a dog's coat by plucking or clipping

Undercoat – The soft, short coat typically concealed by a longer outer coat

Wean – The process through which puppies transition from subsisting on their mother's milk to eating solid food

Whelping – The act of birthing a litter of puppies

Chapter One: Boxer Dog and Its Roots

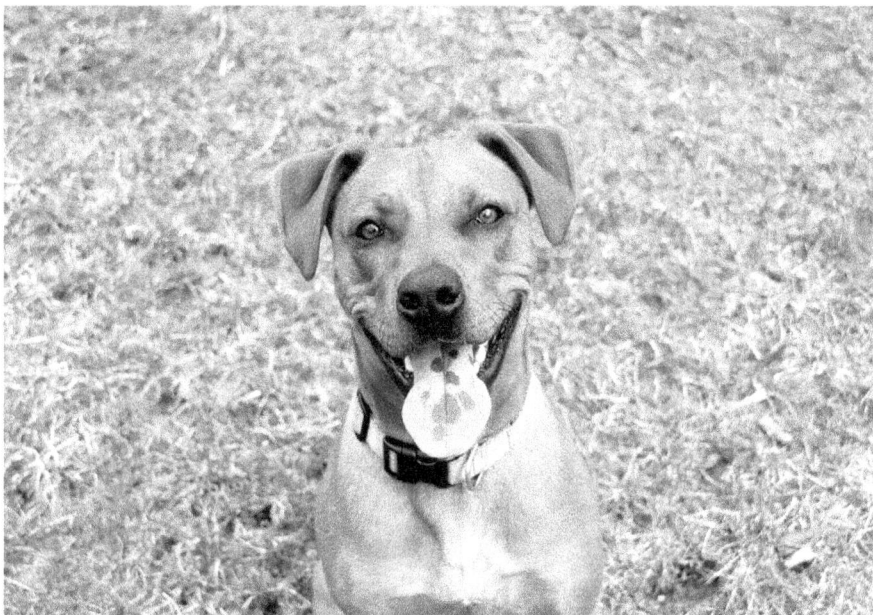

You are about to delve into the beginnings of the Boxer. Here you will discover things you may not know about this sweet and lovingly playful canine. You'll also get to know how they have earned their keep in as army dogs, security canines, therapeutic pets and just all-around "Warmest Most Loving Buddy for All Time."

Their undeniable loyalty and breath-taking exuberance are just some of the many traits of the Boxer which you'll definitely love. You will get to know that each one, whatever similarities they may share, still have distinct personalities from each other.

The next section hopes to shed light and show you the beginnings of its sort and how it has warmed the hearts of many caregivers and guardians.

Facts about Boxer Dogs

The Boxer has a commanding look when it is behaved and sits up in attention. Their expressive eyes can draw your attention and it will be hard to say no to it when it settles its chin on your knee. It can sport various colors and unique patterns. Its white bridle is what sets it apart from other dogs. It has short fur which clings close to its taut skin.

Its jowls hang down the sides of its face almost giving a worried look. During an active play, it will have a wild-eyed look and will have an appearance which seems close to smiling when at play. A happy situation could be as simple as you stepping into your home portal and it would do its own signature happy-dance and personal shimmy.

The slobber-smile is possibly one of the most endearing of the many looks which Boxer guardians miss the most when away from their Boxers. Always on the alert, Boxer dogs are weary of strangers but are not violent with tender patience and a lot of interaction as well as positive reinforcement, the seemingly stubborn Boxer is not difficult at all to train. Working with an experienced successful dog trainer would be something you would want to strongly consider along this road of thinking about getting a Boxer.

One thing is for sure - there will never be a shortage for excitement and fun times with a Boxer around the house. If you are in anyway lacking in sense of humor, the Boxer will definitely teach you to develop a good one!

The History of the Boxer

The Boxer came about in the late 19th century. It is classified as part of the dog group called the Molosser which is also part of the Working Group of canines. A dog of Mastiff descent, the now extinct Bullenbeisser is partly responsible for the much loved Boxer we all love today. For centuries the Bullenbeisser worked as a hunting dog utilized to pursue deer, wild boar and even bear.

The Bullenbeisser would latch onto its prey and hold the prey down until the hunters came. Faster dogs were sought out and so came forth a Bullenbeisser which was smaller. The smaller Bullenbeisser was bred in northern Belgium, in the province of Brabant. It is widely accepted today that the Barbandt Bullenbeisser is an ancestor of the Boxer breed.

It was in 1894 when three Germans came to agreement to stabilize the Boxer's breed and exhibit it at a dog show. Elard König, R. Höpner and Friedrich Robert went on the following year and founded the first Boxers Club in 1896. A detailed document about the Boxers breed standard was first published in 1904 and not much of it has changed up to this very day. It was in the turn of the 20th century when the Boxer was introduced to the United States after making its way through Europe in shows.

In 1904 the American Kennel Club registered the Boxer and in 1915, recognized Dampf vom Dom as the first Boxer Dog Champion. The Boxer was an employed canine during the First World War and acted as a carrier - dog, messenger, guard dog and often times, an attack dog, not until after the Second World War did the Boxer become renowned all over the world. Once the Boxers were taken home by soldiers and a wider audience saw it, the Boxer became an instant hit as a companion, guard dog and quite a show-stopper at dog shows.

Early Genealogy

Munich resident, and German citizen George Alt, crossbred a bridle-colored bitch, Fiora, which came from France, with a dog whose ancestry is unknown but was called "Boxer." The mating resulted in a fawn and white male dog which was called "Lechner's Box" after its caregiver. Lechner's Box was later mated with Fiora and one of its offspring bitch was christened Alt's Schecken. The Schecken was mated with Dr. Toneissen's Tom, who was a Bulldog, and this crossbreeding resulted in the historically significant canine, Mühlbauer's Flocki.

This particular Boxer is significant because it was, Flocki, who was the first one to enter the German Stud Book after being awarded at the St. Bernard's Show in Munich in 1896. It was at the St. Bernard's Show that Boxers were given a specific class.

Flocki's sister, a white bitch called Blanka von Angertor became even more important than her already influential brother when she was mated with the grandson of Lechner's Box, Piccolo von Angertor. This pairing bore Meta von der Passage, a predominantly white bitch considered to be the mother of the breed who played the most important role amongst the original five ancestors. All the sires traced back to her.

She was substantially built and stood low to the ground. It was said that as a producing female of her breed, none can match her record. She was a consistent whelper of marvelous pups of sorts and many of rare quality.

Chapter Two: Boxer Dog Requirements

Boxers are amusing dogs who are an active bunch and who will need lots of stimulation, play, and exercise. There is nothing funnier than seeing this oversized pup-for-life excited about something new, a strange place and new people. Many Boxer guardians will tell you that the Boxer is one canine who likes to have fun and will want you to come along.

Boxers will find a way to get your attention one way or another and this next chapter aims to talk about what to expect when adding a Boxer into your mix. You will also find out about how life may be like when adding a Boxer pup in a home with an established senior Boxer.

They are a sort of canine breed who thrives on your attention and companionship. It is a very rambunctious breed who loves playtime and fun activities with you and other caregivers. Boxers are considered to be a medium-sized dog, which you want to keep in consideration as well.

This canine sort will need you to be there most of the time. If you are one who has to go on out-of-town trips often, put in longs days and nights at work and has ten thousand things to do at once, you may want to think twice about the Boxer as it will need you.

As commanding a stance they may have, Boxers are forever-pups at heart. They may have a loud bark but if socially broken in properly, you will find that the Boxer is a canine who can be trained easily, take instructions, gets along well with others and can be a lifelong pal to you and your Boxer-friendly pets.

Pups of this sort are a playful bunch and love nothing more than to run around and jump about the house or when it gets a chance, to traipse "the wild" outdoors. If you have the sort of household outfitted with expensive things but still in consideration of the Boxer then storage is something you may want to look into because your Boxer may get into too much trouble with caregiver if not.

Do You Need a License?

There are certain regulations and restrictions that should be taken in to consideration when purchasing a dog, or in this case Boxer dog. Acquiring a license for your pets can be different depending on the country, state and region that you are in.

In the United States, there is no federal requirement for getting a license for your pets, but it is the State that regulars these kinds of rules. Though it is not required for you dogs to get a license, it is important that you do so. It will not just provide a protection for your pet, but also to you as a pet owner. An identification number is placed in your dog licensed which is directly linked to your contact details as the owner. This can be very helpful in case your pet gets lost.

It is important to take note that before you can get your dog a license, you must be vaccinated against rabies. This is the only requirement for you to acquire a license. Dog license are renewable every year which means that you have to get another rabies vaccination.

How Many Boxer Dogs Should You Acquire?

A lot! It is advisable to keep one Boxer dog per home. As mentioned in some sections of this chapter, Boxer dog's requires a lot of time and attention when it comes to training. It will be hard for you to train a lot of Boxer dogs. Also, this kind of breed may not be an easy breed for first time dog owners, although some may find it easy to handle. This breed has a thin coat which makes easy to groom.

Owning more than one of any breed is still up to the pet owner since it takes a significant amount of effort in giving them all their needs. Of course, these needs do not only mean that you will provide for their physical daily needs, but also the significant time and affection that is vital for their growth and development. You must be willing to give your best effort in all the aspects of your life when you decide to get a dog.

Do Boxers Get on Well with Other Pets?

Most Boxers will get along well with larger dogs and the smallest of breeds. You will find that with patience and determination, you can make a life out of loving more than one pet.

A Boxer, like most other pets, will have been able to establish a routine and space in the home. If you are introducing a new canine into the home, remember to follow proper guidelines and tips on integrating a new pet into a home with an existing one. One thing is for sure your home will light up with activity and love should this be the route you choose to take.

How to Introduce Your Boxer Dog with Other Pets

Contrary to popular belief, two Boxers in fact get along well famously with each other given the proper guidance and patience during the onset of introduction. If you do decide to have more than one Boxer, you will be opening up your home to a whole lot of fun companionship.

Allow your old canine buddy enough time to get to know the new Boxer on the block. Be sure that you are present with another caregiver to make sure the period of transition is uneventful. Here are some things to remember when considering more than one Boxer.

- Consider the age gap of the senior, established dog and the new one you intend to take in. An established, older Boxer may not find the rambunctiousness of a new pup amusing and make take them some getting used to with each other. In these cases, remember that if your heart is set on this, patience (and the assistance of another caregiver) during integration period is vital.

- Boxers are barkers. They are wired this way. Keep this in mind when considering more than one Boxer. This is also something you want to remember when taking in a younger Boxer with a senior Boxer waiting at home. If the senior Boxer displays tolerance for the smaller dog then you have done a good job of integrating them.

- Space is a huge factor you want to consider when making this decision. Since Boxers are playful and will jump about indoors, it is important that you provide enough living and play space for them to romp around. Be ready to share couch space with them as they do like to lounge with you as you relax. It is important that you, as caregiver, provide them with sufficient indoor and outdoor spaces.

- Make sure you would have provided separate and identical slow-feed bowls and water dishes to avoid overcrowding, and place them in close proximity of each other but separate areas of the same room. This way they can enjoy meals together with a respectable distance between them.

- You will have to work your schedule around to accommodate their needs as they grow. Taking baths, grooming costs or tools, training, and other sundries not only cost money but time. A pet is not self-cleaning, self-feeding or totally independent. Much like a child, you will have to factor in the needs of your Boxer in your daily schedule.

- Unless you've managed to train a Boxer to go potty in the bathroom, you will need to set a scheduled time for natures call. Most people find it ideal to do this twice a day about 2 hours after a meal. Remember that Boxers tend to develop bloating and it is strongly advised that you put off any strenuous activities til it has digested its meal well.

- Provide them with many toys; a soft hypoallergenic blanket they can both share and romp in for a little exercise or a game of Hide and go Seek can be a good source of physical activity for Boxers because they have a penchant for hiding, sneaking up on and playfully lunging at their buddies and guardians. It also is a good nap place alternative for your tuckered out Boxers.

- Aside from sharing a space in your heart, be ready to share your bed as well. Many of these amorous canines are big babies at heart and love nothing more than to snuggle up to you. They are great snugglers and you may often time find yourself clinging on to the edge of your bed or on the floor.

- Romping and running space is a requirement especially for growing pups. If you would like to set some boundaries with your canine, you may opt to get one of those baby fences to discourage it from entering/exiting rooms. As the dog grows you may think about modifying these baby fences. Ideally you should have been able to lay down the law and your Boxer should know it takes its directions from you. Many attest that positive reinforcement is the most effective method of training your Boxers.

- As in most families, conflict may be something you will need to squelch later. When acting as go-between it is advisable to draw their focus from the conflict by clapping loudly and calling out to your warring canine pals.

- Positive reinforcement is encouraged when dealing with Boxers. They are a playful, humorous sort and you will have to extend a whole lot of patience to live harmoniously with one much less two. Punishment in any form after a mistake is not productive to your budding relationship and its growth.

How Much Does A Boxer Cost?

The popularity of the Boxer has risen because of its' loyalty, affection, and the fact that it is a clean dog in terms of self-grooming. However, because some people do not research their possible pets first before taking one in or acquiring one, many are not ready for the boisterousness the Boxer brings to the family. If you have a big heart and are fortunate enough to adopt one, consider yourself lucky. You will want to investigate the history of the canine before doing so to be on the up and up of what to expect.

Boxers can cost anywhere from $300-$3000. Why the wide margin you may ask. This is when your research skills come in when looking for a reputable breeder. There are unscrupulous pet farms that pay no mind to the breeding process and breeds for the sole purpose of profit hence the price will be considerably low. They are not concerned about the history of either dogs or mass produce to meet a need with no regard for future wellbeing of the dog. Stay away from that sort.

Pups from upstanding breeders would have been dewormed and would have had its initial inoculation from the vet. Ideally, the pup should be with its mother til after weaning. Reputable breeders will ask you questions and a lot of it, if they are worth their water. Breeders of this sort may ask you a little about your living conditions to make sure the pairing is suitable for both parties. They may ask you questions that will reveal if you are ready to take in a Boxer.

Remember that Boxers if not bred properly can live with serious medical problems passed on by sick parents. Save yourself the heartache and stay away from pet farms. Find yourself a reputable breeder by asking Boxer guardians, as well vets and Boxer clubs in the area. If your heart is set on getting a Boxer, get ready to wait. It's like anticipating a baby! Reputable breeders do not have pups on hand. After a breeder and you agree then mating will commence. This screening procedure somehow assures the breeder that the Boxer is going to a good home. Another red flag you must look out for is the price of the pup. The more expensive it is the more care was put into the pups. It is up to you to ask the right questions at this time and ask if you can visit the facilities. Ask questions too. You will need vital information to assure your furry pal a long, healthy, happy life.

This aims to help you find out if you are financially ready to take on the responsibility of being caregiver to a Boxer. You'll read an overview of what to expect in terms of cost of its care and upkeep. Here you will find out about the average cost of food, treats and toys, vet and medical care, sleep and carrying equipment as well as other sundries your Boxer will need.

Initial Costs

Expect to pay a four-figure sum to a reputable breeder and sit patiently. No breeder of good repute will have pups on hand and if a "breeder" does this should be an immediate red flag. As with other pedigrees, Boxers if not bred properly will be susceptible to medical conditions that will cost heartache, unnecessary illnesses, time and money.

Avoid this dark path and take the high road and wait for your Boxer as you oversee the process of pairing, mating, delivery and nursing period. Better yet, visit your local pet shelter and rescue one who is in need of your nurturing care instead.

You initial budget should include neutering, inoculation, vet visit, grooming supplies, toys, equipment, and food. Your emotional budget should be overflowing with love and compassion for the animal you are getting too.

Make sure that you are allowed to see the pups with its mother and its surroundings. No upstanding breeder will deny of this as they should be as concerned as you are in ensuring the pup(s) a good, well-balanced life with you.

A good comparison of taking in or acquiring a Boxer is that it is almost like having a baby. There are areas where the comparisons stops but this should give you an idea of what it would take and cost to add one to the household. Taking in a Boxer and adding it to the family mix is almost equal to being responsible for a child. These are things as you have to consider when choosing the breed of pet best suited for your family and your finances.

As you might have noticed, a range of prices were provided here. It is up to you on how creative you are with some of the other things that you can make at home and save a bundle.

You will want to invest on some of equipment your canine will be using year in and year out, like its bed and slow-feeding dishes.

Training Cost

You can scout around for reputably successful Boxer trainers. Make sure to be available for these trainings as the trainings are as much for you as it is for your Boxer. There are some equipment you can fashion yourself if you are one who is handy with tools, like the crate, and fence. Savings you gain from making your own sturdy equipment (fence, crate, leash, car restrain) can go toward the more essential needs of your buddy like yearly vet bills, inoculations and boarding/pet hotel fees.

Boarding Cost

Factor in yearly lodging fees for your Boxer if you are the sort of family who goes on long trips out of town or out of the country. You will not be able to bring your Boxer with a lot of freedom if you fly to your vacations. However, do bring your lovingly playful Boxer with you if you plan to take a quick weekend camping trip or a hike out in the woods. You'll see a whole new side of your new friend in "wild" surroundings. Loyalty and alertness is what the Boxer brings in these situations.

However, because of the Boxers' short fur it is not advisable for it to be out in the elements for too long without some sort of protection whether against cold or warmth. Remember to do this when it is not too hot or too cold.

Costs Overview

Requirements	Cost
Purchase Price (puppy)	Starts at $1000, show dog price will be considerably higher.
Yearly Inoculation	around $100
Yearly Vet Bill	around $400
Spay/Neuter (one time)	$400
Food (yearly)	$500 and up
Dog Bed	$75 - $100
Treats and Chew Bones	$75 - $100

Bowl	$25
Collar	$25
Leash	$25
Training	$150 - $200
Fence	$750 - $1,500
Heartworm	$50 - $100
Boarding	$50 - $200
Grooming Tools	$50 - 200
Crate	$50 - $150
Car Restrain	$75 - $100
Approximate Total Cost	$3,800 - $5,125

What Are The Pros and Cons of a Boxer?

The Boxer is a boisterously playful canine that stays a puppy at heart most of its life. It shows how happy and excited it can be when it is. It will run at breakneck speed around the house and get into all sorts of funny, minor mishaps that can be amusing. To avoid accidents remember to dog proof your home.

The Boxer needs its space to run around and be silly. It needs attention and interaction. You will have to be as active at it is to be able to keep up with it. You will have to show your Boxer who gives the orders around the house and it may seem stubborn at first but with time and patience you will notice a shift in its recognition of hierarchy of command.

The Pros of Owning a Boxer

This breed…

- is playful

- integrates well with its caregivers

- loves company

- enjoys interaction with its guardians

- is friendly and sociable with most pets smaller or bigger than it

- makes all sorts of funny bodily noises

- will capture your heart with its soulful eyes that have a slight worried look to it

- is able to do the kidney bean dance

- is a good cuddler

- is a big baby in a fun way

The Cons of Owning a Boxer

This breed…

- runs at top speed around the house

- tends to jump about on furniture

- is more prone to some medical conditions than other canines.

Chapter Three: Purchasing a Boxer Dog

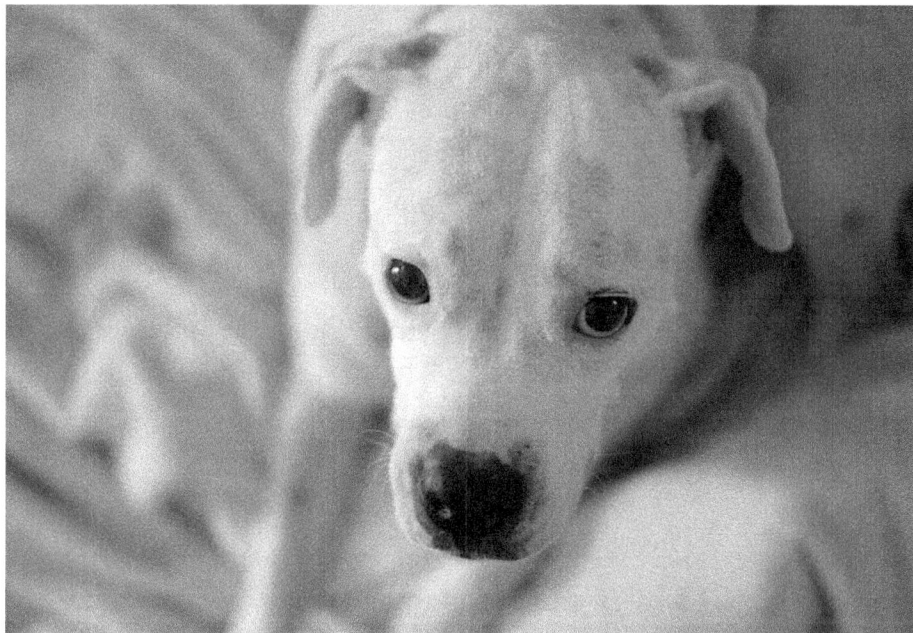

As with other pedigreed pets, Boxers in our present society, should be produced in an ethically humane manner that will lessen the likelihood of medical conditions the canine is prone to if bred in a thoughtless, haphazard manner. Acquiring a pet is not easy carefree as it may seem. It requires patience, care, knowledge of the animal's weaknesses and strengths, as well as how to give it the proper nurturing to allow it to live a long and happy life. You will find useful tips and things to look out for whilst on the quest of adding a Boxer to your home. Keep in mind that the method of breeding of the canine will affect its health.

Where Should You Acquire a Boxer?

There will be a number of options presented to a possible Boxer guardian on how to acquire one. It is advised by the author that the reader do homework and research the process of the breeders you will deal with as you seek out your Boxer. If your options are limited to a pet shop, you want to ask questions about how the pup was bred. Walk away if they are not able to answer you these questions. This indicates that the sole intention of selling the pups is to profit from a sale. There is no regard of the breeding method of the pups which may pose a great problem in the canine's life later.

Do consider adopting a Boxer. Not only would you be saving a hefty amount of money you'll also have the loving loyalty and amusing antics of the Boxer to keep you company. Ask around your local community. Your neighborhood-vet may have information and could give you leads on where to look. Just remember the points below as you chose which option fits you best.

Upstanding Breeders

Grade A breeders will have all pertinent information on a pup and you are ideally part of most of the process of mating. Paying top dollar can be an indication of the care and attention given to the pup. You are assured of that only ethical methods are employed during the process. Provided that all goes well, you should have a happy, healthy pup complete with initial inoculation and vet care.

Giving access to future Boxer guardians to check out the breeder's facilities is a good indication of transparency and any breeder who is open to receiving your presence is a breeder you would want to strongly consider. They will be able to provide you with history of both parents and papers to support their claim. You, as well, should be furnished with all the initial papers necessary to acquire your own furry buddy. Check out breeders websites if possible and research their reputation. This is true too for other avenues you may consider taking as you continue on your quest to seek out your perfectly imperfect Boxer companion.

Experienced Boxer Guardians

You may want to look at your local community ads and check that path out as well. Someone may be moving out and can't take their Boxer with them and will need a new loving home. Again ask about the history of the canine before closing any deals. Be sure that when dealing with either a breeder or a Boxer guardian that all papers and records are sorted out and available for your own files.

Boxer guardians should provide you with complete papers of training and medical certifications, license and inoculation records. The upside to this path is that you will be taking in a Boxer who you have information on and with all necessary papers available to you. You are also at an advantage if you are able to see the Boxer with its current guardians and see how it interacts around its humans.

Pet Rescue / Shelters

As with previous Boxer owners and upstanding breeders so should you be if you choose to rescue from a shelter. This route is a little tricky and you should be aware that if the history of the dog is not available then you will possibly be spending more in medical costs and vet fees. And even if information is available it may be very limited.

Bless your heart if you are in strong consideration of adopting from a rescue or shelter. You should however be aware that not all information you need to secure a healthy future for the canine is assured, so unless you are financially capable and ready to provide for it wholeheartedly you might want to take another route of acquisition.

The upside to this is that a Boxer who has had a previous caregiver has possibly had, at the very least, minimal training and will require just a bit of time in orienting itself with its new surroundings.

Remember to make a lot of space for it prior to the day you welcome your rescue Boxer home and be ready for a lot of breakneck speed sprints as it will definitely display excitement in its curiosity.

You will be surprised at the generosity of affection a Boxer can shower its caregivers and how much love and care it can revert back to you. Their grateful smiles and somber smiles will be more than enough to make your heart explode with love for this always young-at-heart, perpetual puppy.

What to Remember When Choosing a Reputable Boxer Breeder

Right off the bat, make certain that you are dealing with reputable, experienced and upstanding breeders/Boxer caregivers. This is vital to your Boxers health and well - being.

Here are some tips on seeking out an upstanding Boxer breeder:

- Network and be in contact with groomers, pet shops and. Network with groomers, pet shelters, veterinary clinics and experienced Boxer caregivers.

- Research humane and ethical manners of breeding procedures. Check out breeders with websites and study their reputation, ranking and license.

- Do not hesitate to ask questions. And ask lots of them. Don't be taken for a ride and be armed with information you have researched and studied.

- Ask about the methods the breeders employ from canine selection, mating procedure, before and after birth living conditions. You can even ask to make visits to the facilities to see the conditions of the animals.

- Eliminate "breeders" and contacts who give flowery, shady, dodgy and uninformed answers. Make certain that you are only dealing with the most upstanding in their field to avert avoidable heartache and costly medical bills.

- If the breeders are not able to give you straightforward answers, walk away. Dealing with a shady breeder adds stress to you and takes away the joyful anticipation of your new buddy. You want to bring home and introduce a healthy pup or dog to your home so make sure that you give the answers you need. An honest answer of no known history is better than an ill pup being passed of as healthy.

- Drive out and drop in on the breeder's facilities if you are given permission. You want to look out for the surroundings and its sanitation. When a breeder is happy to give you information and offers up more important bits that you should know, you should strongly keep this breeder in consideration.

- Payment and fees will be talked about so don't forget what terms the breeder has to offer. You can then make a payment to secure your Boxer. Breeders of upstanding repute will be more than welcoming when you ask to visit your pup once it has arrived.

List of Websites of Breeders and Rescue Adoption

Below is the list of the websites of Boxer Dog breeders and rescues.

Boxer Breeders

AKC Puppy Finder

<marketplace.akc.org/puppies/boxer>

Puppy Spot

<https://www.puppyspot.com/breed/boxer/>

Rescue Adoption

RescueLA

<https://www.boxer-rescue-la.com/>

Adopt a Boxer

<https://www.adoptaboxerrescue.com/>

Atlanta Boxer Rescue

Adopt a Pet

<www.adoptapet.com/s/adopt-a-boxer>

The Boxer Rescue of Oklahoma

<www.tbro.org/avaliableboxer>

PA Boxers

Legacy Boxers

Carolina Boxer Rescue

Chapter Four: How to Select a Healthy Boxer Dog

This chapter aims to carefully show the reader what you need to look out for, measures you need to take and what you should and shouldn't do to keep your Boxer in a happy healthy disposition.

You have already read about conditions it can be prone to and measures you can take to avoid the avoidable. This section enumerates more ways to ensure you bring home a healthy Boxer that will share many playful years with you.

Pets are creatures that depend on you for their daily needs of nurturing, nutrition and love. It will be up to you to know what to do in events of emergencies and unplanned situations. You need to be able to recognize signs that display discomfort. Your pet will be counting on you as its guardian and caregiver. This is why it is imperative that possible pet owners in consideration of adopting or acquiring a pet needs to do the proper research to ensure a transition which is smooth and snag-free.

It is important that you and other caregivers it may have known the important part you all play in the health and well - being of your Boxer buddy. The more you empower yourself with information needed to raise it well the chances of it living a healthy existence exponentially heightens. Research also gives you a better edge on knowing what to expect when expecting your Boxer.

How to Select a Healthy Boxer When Buying

A Boxer is known to live a long healthy life of up to 12-14 years if given the right attention, medical care and provided with proper nutrition for its sort. You have already read about the possible medical conditions it can be prone to - whether genetically transmitted or developed - and you are encouraged to ask your local vet for more information you may need to avert the incidence of illness.

Make the transition of moving in for your Boxer an easy one and allow it time to integrate itself into its new surroundings.

Behavior around Humans

It is weary of strangers but sociable, if a Boxer displays distress or is jumpy then it may have undergone abuse and or experienced neglect from its previous caregivers. You may have to put in more than a bit of time in integrating your new Boxer should this is the case. However, with time and loving patience, the new Boxer will come to see that you only mean good toward it and will eventually warm up to you. Keep in mind that they are the most content in your presence and thrive best in an atmosphere of a loving environment.

Mobility

Check out its present living conditions. If you are not allowed to do so, then this may be a red flag. You want to make sure that the canine is living in a clean environment and that the dog is mobile with no broken limbs. You want to look out for signs of lethargy. You want to make sure that the canine has no problems moving, running and jumping about. Lack thereof could be indication of injury which any future guardian should know.

Tail and ears

Docking and cropping became controversial and continues to be such. Tail docking depends on the dogs size, whether it is predominantly an inside or outside dog. If the dog is predominantly indoors you can opt to forego docking. Docking and cropping is done to a Boxer to avoid nicks on its ears and injury to its tail when at play or when they run. Ideally docking is non-surgical procedure done at 3-5 days of the pups life. Cropping is said to be an unnecessary procedure and is more for cosmetic appearances. Should you decide to have your Boxers' ears cropped it should ideally be done within 8-12 weeks of its life. Any later will cause memorable pain to the canine and can be avoided.

Pet Interaction

It will be necessary for you and another caregiver to be present during the period of introduction to a family with existing pets. One way to see how your new Boxer pup will integrate itself to its new family is to see it in its natural surroundings. Seeing the pup interact with its present caregivers and other animals is a good way of determining how the transition will go. It will also provide you an insight on how to adjust if need be. Your investment of time and patience during this period is crucial to a happy, hassle-free transition. You will need to make time for this milestone to be a successful one. Be sure that you have provided it with enough romping space and that you have removed all valuables you don't want shattered.

Appetite

Boxers are pretty fast eaters and can wolf down meals in a flash. If you do not take measure to control how they eat their meals they may suffer from stomach upset or worse, canine bloat. If your pup shows a healthy appetite this is a good indicator of good health.

Body Appearance

Scrutinize and examine its body, its fur, skin, ears, tail, legs, limbs, underbelly and joints. If they show any discomfort from gentle checking you should investigate on why it is so

Coat

The Boxers short fur makes looking for fleas or ticks easier to spot. Should they have a case of the fleas then it will be advisable to get rid of the problem before bringing your Boxer home.

Skin

Boxers are prone to acne and sunburn. The dog's skin should be free from bald spots, patches, rashes and bumps. Check for any signs of this and have them treated if present on the canine.

Eyes

The somber looking eyes of the Boxer should be bright and lively, clear and discharge free. Boxers have expressive eyes that are hard to resist once you lock sights.

Ears

Clean ears are wax and dirt free. Watch out for tiny nicks or wounds that may get infected and provide treatment if any is found to avoid infection. You can clean the ears of a Boxer using a mixture of baking soda and water. With a soft cloth wipe the inside of the ears gently. Do not introduce a cotton bud in its ears as this may cause eardrum damage.

Mouth and Teeth

The Boxers jaw slightly protrudes but you should check for any deformities that may be present.

Belly or Stomach

Check for lumps or swollenness around the stomach area. None should be present.

Anal Area

You want to check that the hygiene of the pup is assured. One way of doing that is to check its anal area.

Reminder:

Upstanding breeders only release Boxer pups at 12 weeks. It is strongly advised though that separation from mother is kept off until the pup has weaned off the dam. Wait until the puppy is ready to eat solid dog food until you take your Boxer home.

Chapter Five: The Food and Nourishment Needs of Your Boxer Dog

The well-being and future health of your Boxer greatly depends on you and what you feed it. As a guardian the task of choosing the proper foods falls on you. At the beginning you may have to experiment and find out which foods suit your Boxer best, try introducing different meat-based foods to them.

You will find many different options available to you in the market. Make certain that you study up on ingredients that are good and bad as well as non - essential for your new buddy. Make it a habit to read labels and find out about ingredients used to make the food, if you choose to feed it commercially made dog food. Should you prefer to feed it raw, and then find out what you should be feeding it and what amounts you should serve per meal to meet your Boxer's nutritional needs.

This section of the book aims to help you decide on how and what to feed your Boxer pal. It will give you tips and reminders of what to include and what to avoid when preparing meals for your furry buddy.

The Nutritional Needs of a Boxer

Like most four-legged pets, canine or feline, Boxers are carnivores and need meat in their daily diet. As a potential guardian you want to find out what you should be feeding your Boxer to ensure it a long, healthy and balanced life. Nutritionally sound food is essential to any living beings' growth and wellness. This is not an expense you want to scrimp on and you have to be ready for the long run financial cost.

See Chapter Nine of this book and be reminded about the medical condition Boxers are prone to when they over eat or eat too fast.

Bloat is a very serious Boxer problem that can be avoided by training your dog to eat slowly. Encourage slow feeding by introducing a slow-feed bowl to your pup and replace it with a larger slow-feeding bowl as it grows. This goes the same for drinking, be sure to keep your canine buddy well hydrated throughout the day to discourage big gulps of thirst.

Check out slow feeding equipment and sundries your canine will be using for a long time to come and invest in them. Equipment which is a bit more expensive usually reflects the quality of materials used and care put into them. Again, research is vital to finding out what products are durable, long lasting and sturdy. Your Boxer dog is after all the playful one and a perpetual teenager-at-heart. Read on and find out about what to put in those bowls.

Feeding Your Four-Week Old Pup

An upstanding breeder will only release a pup after it has weaned off its dam or 12 weeks after its birth. This

allows the pup enough time to nourish of its mother and
prepared for solid foods.

Solid foods should be slowly introduced at 4 weeks
old. At a slow and steady pace, start giving your Boxer pup
a little bit of solid food - with a base of what you have been
feeding its dam. At this stage of the pups' life you want to
give it food that you have softened or mushed with a milk-
replacer.

Feeding Your Eight-Week Old Boxer

Feeding and nutrition will be vital during this period
of your Boxers growth spurt. Your Boxer will be growing
exponentially fast during this time and it will need proper
feeding to ensure its overall good health. By this time, your
little Boxer buddy should be used to solid foods.

To ensure good health do not randomly feed your
Boxer. Instead schedule its feedings. This prevents over
feeding and helps discipline your pup as it grows. Studies
have shown that a canine on a schedule is better behaved.
For pups 8 weeks to 8 months, it is best to give those 3 meals
a day. Many Boxer guardians find it easier to set the same

feeding schedule for the humans and the family and their pets. Try this method and see if it works for you.

Feeding Your Growing Boxer

As your Boxer works its way toward a year old of puppyhood, you may reduce the number of times you give it meals down to twice a day. You want to factor in treats and rewards you give to it throughout the day. Never feed it outside of its schedule unless giving it a treat for good behavior, and do not feed it food that you eat, especially any leftovers from your meals. Keep in mind that the Boxer is prone to bloating and this condition can be absolutely avoided.

What to Feed a Boxer

Now that your Boxer is ready to go on solid food, you need to decide how to best feed it. If you choose to give it commercially made, store bought dog food, be sure that you choose only the best quality. Remember to read ingredient labels and learn what go into making the product. There are way too many substandard dog food brands in the market that you want to avoid. Again, ensuring the good health of your Boxer hangs on the sort of food you give to it.

Commercial Food

Many store bought brands have "fillers". These could be by-products of an animal or extenders like soy or corn. Meat by-product can be any unused part of an animal (chicken beak, cow hoof, pig nose, fowl) to create meat products for human consumption. Road kill and animals which died in transit can also be part of this mix. Be wary when you read a label that says "meat-products". Soy and corn are also commonly used as extenders and have been known to contain allergens that may be bad for or contain no nutritional value to your Boxer. A lot of commercially made dog food contains food additives and coloring as well which you want to stay away from as these can be cause for allergic reactions and bad for your Boxers health.

Now is the time to research what to feed your dog. You may accomplish this by asking experienced Boxer guardians, veterinarians, as well as upstanding breeders. They would have had enough experience to be able to shed some light on this important factor of your canine's health.

Home Cooked Meals

Home cooked meals not only allow you quality control of the sort of food your Boxer is getting, it also will save you money in the long haul. Cooking meals for your Boxer would be ideal if you have the time to do this. Many Boxer caregivers find cooking for the Boxer as they cook meals for the family not only saves them time and money, it also lets the guardian monitor the sort of nutrition being given the growing Boxer.

Meats

The prime ingredient of your Boxers meal should be 35-40% fresh, quality, wholesome meat. Tuna or Mackerel fish, a lean chicken breast, veal, lamb, turkey, lean hamburger, lamb. Should you opt to raw feed your Boxer dog you will have to be more mindful of the freshness and quality of the meat products.

Vegetables

Remember to include good vegetables acceptable for a Boxer diet. 25-30% of the meal should consist of one or two servings of raw or boiled sweet peas, potatoes, carrots, string beans, steamed broccoli, cauliflower, and sweet potatoes.

Carbohydrates

You will want to add in a little bit of starch to your Boxer's meals. A little bit of rice or a few pieces of boiled pasta would do the job of loading up on much needed energy that your Boxer will need.

Water

Always remember to hydrate your Boxer as it is not built to self-regulate its body temperature. On hot days, especially on a foray out, be sure to have had your Boxer have a good drink of water and bring along a bottle of water for it. So goes the same for meals. Remember that Boxers will experience medical problems should it drink or eat too fast. One way of avoiding greedy slurping and gobbling is to follow a strict feeding schedule and to set out fresh water so as your buddy can grab a quick drink anytime of the day.

Treats

Treats should be given as reward for good behavior and not at random. Choose the best quality treats that will have nutritional value to your furry buddy. There are treats that have ingredients that are of no value to your canine and may cause unwanted weight gain.

Stick to a Schedule

Your feisty little Boxer may not know it yet but you play a big role in its young, budding life. Like us humans, pets too thrive on certain routine and scheduled activities as much as they live for spontaneity and all things new.

Keep a schedule for necessary things like grooming (brushing, tooth brushing, bathing, cleaning ears, and trimming nails), eating and outside playtime. Sticking to a routine allows your dog to learn to become comfortable in situations they would otherwise find uncomfortable or unpleasant (grooming) as well as give them the discipline to lead a healthy life and avoid health problems (given the proper feeding amount at fixed periods throughout the day).

Chapter Six: Maintenance for Your Boxer Dogs

The beauty and clumsy elegance of the Boxer is truly endearing. In spite of its playful awkwardness during fun time and its seemingly "ill" manners of loud burps and obnoxious farts, it is still by far one of the cleanest dogs you will come across. It is quite well known for being a self-cleaning beast, which is another of its more endearing qualities. Comparable to the agility of a cat cleaning itself, the Boxer is just as skilled in self-cleaning.

It is known to have a woodsy nutty smell to it that most if not all Boxer guardians would attest to be true.

Cleaning Your Boxer's Ears and Eyes

Boxers if unscrupulously bred could be prone to deafness. It is important that you as caregiver know this to avoid any injury to it. To clean your Boxer's ears, dip a soft cloth in a mild solution of baking soda and water and gently rub its ears from the inside out. Do not attempt to introduce cotton buds or Q-tips to clean the inside of its ears as this may cause avoidable hearing impairment to your canine. It is best to seek the help of your vet if you are unsure of how to do this. You can watch your vet do it and later on clean your Boxer's ears exactly how they did.

Remember that you want to clean your Boxer's eyes as well. With the same gentle strokes, clean the eyes of your Boxer with a soft, moist cloth.

Grooming Your Boxer

Brushing your Boxer will be one of the easiest tasks you will need to do which you can incorporate during downtime or in between playtime. Fortunately, with the Boxers close to the skin coat, it will be a breeze getting this bit of necessity done. Having shorter fur, the Boxer isn't prone to matting or tangling like other canines. This will also be a good time to check your Boxers skin condition and investigate for acne, ticks, fleas, rash, nick, spot or discoloration.

Bathing Your Boxer

Remember that the Boxer is perhaps one of the cleanest dogs around so bathing the dog twice or thrice a month is within reasonable limits. If you're Boxer gets too muddy or dirty during leash-free time and you determine that it does need a bath, have it sit in a tub filled with warm water and wet its skin thoroughly. Lather on pet-approved shampoo and never substitute your shampoo to clean your Boxer as it may develop avoidable skin conditions.

Once you've given it a good scrubbing rinse and wash off the shampoo lather with warm water. Make certain that no remaining suds are left on the skin as you rinse your Boxer off with warm water. Once it has shaken off excess water give it a good rub down and towel dry your buddy.

During cold weather it is advisable to use warm water and a soft cloth to wash off any dirt, mud or grime your Boxer may have picked up.

Trimming Your Boxers' Nails

Your Boxer is going to be a boisterous one so trimming its paw nails can cause anxiety in the canine. Exposing your Boxer to this necessary routine is best when it is young. Having it grow up knowing this is a necessary routine and is part of its grooming process. To be able to successfully integrate this grooming bit to your canine you want start introduction of nail trimming when it is a pup. You may use nail file to start it off and as it grows introduce more efficient tools to get the job done. It will not be an easy job to do but it is something that your dog can get used to with your patience.

Choosing the right tool that will get the job done is one thing you will have to experiment with. But take great caution when doing so. A Boxer when nicked in the quick can profusely bleed and may require healing.

The guillotine cutter puts pressure on and beneath the nail. A clipper does the same job only with pressure applied on either side of the nail. You've got files to file down its nails but may prove ineffective as the canine grows and its nails toughen. There are pet paw-nail grinders available in the market however as the canine grows, experienced Boxer guardians have found that pet nail grinders does not get the same results than if you were to utilize a grinder. Check out your tool shed and dig up a rotary grinder or invest in one - you will thank yourself for it later.

Rotary Grinders

You will probably have to go through a few nail clipping tools before you find one agreeable to your Boxer. Once you determine what it is that your pal is comfortable in using, invest in that. Rotary grinders seem to be one tool that the Boxer fusses very little over. Some guardians like to use stone grinders but find that the grinding of the stone against the canines nails become hot after a while.

There are fine- or medium-grit sanding band grinds that do not heat up as fast but does not sit too well with a Boxer as compared to a stone grinder. Remember that if you decide to use a stone or sand bands, always move the tool in a circular motion careful to not keep it one place for too long.

Test different options and see if you can have a professional do each session for you with a guardian or yourself present. Note and observe which method meets the least resistance - and resistance you will experience - and from there employ the same method at home.

This procedure would be a little easier if another guardian was present to help out as the continuous vibration of the grinder may bother your Boxer. If you choose to use a guillotine or a clipper, expose the nail of the canine and cut a little above the quick (the fleshy under part of the nail). Be sure that you do not nick the flesh as Boxers are prone to bleeding from their nails.

Proper Oral Hygiene for Your Boxer Dog

Brushing Your Boxer's Tooth

Show me an animal who enjoys brushing and we'd have seen the 1% of the minority of pets who enjoy a good mouth cleaning. However unpopular this activity is, it something that you will need to mind because like most pets - and humans - your Boxer will be prone to health problems if proper oral hygiene is not practiced.

For successful future tooth brushing, start off your Boxer while it is a pup. Incorporating grooming practices early allows your new Boxer to get used to these activities and become routine.

Choose the proper toothbrush and dog-approved toothpaste on your new buddy. Substituting dog toothpaste for human toothpaste will introduce chemicals that could be toxic to your furry pal. Brushing twice or thrice a week is good however, although daily brushing would still be ideal.

Chews

Dog chews are ideal to help keep your Boxers mouth clean. Major benefits have been derived from using quality dental chews. Tartar, plaque and food bits are removed with the chewing action and does a really good job of keeping a canine's mouth clean. Grade A chews keep the Boxers breath smelling fresh and keeps from future buildup of food-debris.

Make sure you look up the ingredients used in making the chews as some can contain fat and excessive calories your Boxer will not need.

Food

The overall nutrition of any living being hinges on the quality of food intake, a balanced diet, and the amount and manner of consumption. Introduce quality food that will allow the canine to thrive and live a healthy life. Remember to give it the nutritional needs it requires. A healthy dog grows with healthy teeth.

Is the next chapter we shall discuss the nutritional needs and foods you should give your new canine for it to thrive.

Habitat Requirements for Boxer Dogs

The great thing about Boxer dogs is that they don't take up too much space to roam around with even if they seem like a big dog, but aside from space, the main thing your Boxer needs in terms of its habitat is lots of love and affection from his human companions and adequate daily exercise. Even though the boxer is sometimes too stubborn and can be witty, it is a very loyal and affectionate breed that bonds closely with family, so you should make an effort to spend some quality time with your Boxer breed each and every day. If you're dog doesn't get enough attention he may be more likely to develop problem behaviors like chewing or excessive barking and potential aggression as well as separation anxiety.

In addition to playing with your Boxer dog and spending time with him every day, you also need to make sure that his needs for exercise are met. The Boxer breed doesn't require extensive exercises but it is still recommended to take your dog for a walk or run once in a while plus some active play time, this is very important for your Boxer dog. You should also make sure your that he gets plenty of mental stimulation from interactive toys and games.

Toys and Accessories for Boxer Dogs

Boxer breeds' supplies will change as each young puppy matures into an adult dog and then yet again when then also when they become a senior. The products associated with Boxer dogs clearly indicate if they're appropriate for their age. When you are already ready to welcome your new Boxer into your home, make sure you already have their personal supplies stocked to help keep them happy and healthy at every stage of their lives.

With the right nutrients and ingredients, Boxer's food supplies can help give your dog the building blocks they need to prolong their years of face licking and tail wagging. You can also provide your dog's treats to keep them feeling rewarded, focused and excited to learn new tricks and right manners.

However, if your Boxer's aren't pleased by treats, you can give them a collection of dog toys for every preference. In that way, you can have a reward system for your dog or simply just give them some much needed exercise with their plush dog ball or toys.

In addition to treating and toy fueled playtime, daily walks with your Boxers' accessories can provide great bonding moments. There is a large array of Boxer's accessories and clothes for every occasion and season to keep them looking comfortably stylish wherever they go.

If your Boxer's are new to walks, there are also specialized dog accessories that are already available to help leash train your Boxer's, so you can make sure your young puppies can respect the rules of the road as they explore the world outside of their homes. There are also dog training supplies available in the market to reinforce good behavior like pee pads, clickers, and bark collars.

Additionally, your dog deserves the best bed or crating dog supplies for their size and sleeping style. Dog crate covers, heated bed products, and blankets can also make for a more comfortable good night's rest.

For your on-the-go needs of your dogs, there are also dog carriers and car seat accessories available in the market if you want to make trips to the park. Getting the right car accessories for your Boxer pet doesn't just only make you hassle-free during travel, but they will also make it more comfortable and safer too.

Also, if your vet prescribes or recommends something for your pup, you must really invest on it like dog products to tackle fleas, ticks, and more.

Keeping Your Boxer Dogs Indoors and Outdoors

Boxer dogs are indoor dogs so they must always be kept inside our homes, in a safely fenced yard, or on-leash. But of course, they are not supposed to be inside your house all the time. They can still go for a walk at the dog park provided they have a full supervision. This section will enumerate the tips that will help your dog stay happy whether indoors or outdoors.

Just like other pets, Boxer dogs like to see the outside world (they're creatures after all) so why not open the curtains of your homes so they can have a foresight on the outside. Most dogs enjoy a nice view, especially when it's sunny outside, the incoming light can improve your dog's mood. Open also the windows so that your pet can get some fresh air. But make sure to do this only if you are at home and there's someone to look after your dog. You can also try buying a treadmill for your Boxer dogs. It can be a great way to keep your dogs in good shape when you have no time to exercise them.

Your dog then can definitely exercise at home when it's convenient whether you are sick or the weather is bad. Having a bond with your dog indoors is the best thing to do when you can't go outside for a walk. Make sure to always make time for your Boxer pets. You may snuggle on the couch, make a brushing session, or even a massage will definitely keep them happy. You can also practice training your dog when you are inside your homes. Although it may seem boring, your Boxer dogs might enjoy this because it gives them a job and they are getting to work with you. Taking even just a small amount of time to practice tricks, obedience, etc. will keep your dog's mind sharp and will eliminate boredom.

As mentioned earlier, Boxer dogs are intended in indoors so it is not really recommended that he should be treated as an outdoor dog, even though he can moderately tolerate the hot and cold weather. So it's better off leaving him inside your home with your family.

You can let your Boxer dogs go outdoors like in the yard when he already reached eight weeks old. However, make sure that there are no other dogs that can get in and this includes other dogs you own. Make sure also that your yard is clean and that you have treated the ground for weeds and fleas. When your pet reached eight weeks old, you can take them outside for as long as you hold him at all times. His feet can never touch the ground outside until he has had all the necessary shots except in your back yard if it is safe.

You must avoid taking your dogs out in public areas until his puppy shots are already completed. This includes walking along the footpath, being out in your front yard, at the shops, in parks, in yards belonging to neighbours and so on. Your Boxer dogs must be 10 -12 weeks old before he can be safely taken outdoors but be sure you still have his leash at all times.

It's very unhealthy to keep your dog indoors at all times. Your home won't have sufficient space for him to roam around unless you have a spacious mansion. It is necessary to give your Boxer pets a small amount of sunshine each day for Vitamin D. Besides, getting enough exercise for your pets is very essential. You have to plan your walks the same time each day so that he has something to look forward to. Exercises are important because it helps him get off diseases and he could be able to smell, hear and see new things. This makes his hearth healthy and balances out his muscle tone.

Chapter Seven: Showing Your Boxer Dog

In order to show your Boxer dog you have to make sure that he meets the requirements for the breed standard and you need to learn the basics about showing dogs.

In this chapter you will receive information about the breed standard for Boxer breeds and you will find general information about preparing your dog for show.

Boxer Dog Breed Standard

Appearance

According to the American Kennel Club breed standards, in order for the canine to be recognized as a full-fledged Boxer, the dog needs to have a head in perfect proportion to its body. Another breed standard dictates that the highest importance lies on the muzzle being correctly formed in proportion with its skull. Breed standard hangs on the balance of the length of the muzzle to its whole head - standard is 1:3 in length and 2:3 of the width. The fold is visibly present beginning from tip of the nose which runs downward on both sides of its muzzle. The nose, too, in keeping with proportions should be a tad higher than the root of its muzzle. The Boxer, completing its overall facial features is to sport a protruding jaw and have a mild under bite.

Head

The unique stamp of individuality of the Boxer is its chiseled head. The head has to be in proper proportion with the canine's body. Its blunt, broad muzzle is a feature which is distinct. High value is placed on its muzzle being of proper form and is balanced with its skull.

Special attention is devoted to the head during judging. General appearance and overall balance is given great consideration. After scrutiny of the head, other body components are checked for the proper construction, and the canine's gait is studied for efficiency.

Skull

- Top of the skull should be slightly arched not rounded or noticeably broad

- Occiput is not too pronounced

- Forehead displays slight indentation between the eyes and forms a distinct stop on the muzzles topline

- Cheeks should be flat and not bulge; maintaining clean lines of the skull as cheeks taper into the muzzle

Muzzle and Nose

- Must be proportionately developed in length, width, and depth

- Shape of muzzle is influenced by both jaw bones, teeth and placement of lips

- Top of muzzle shouldn't slant downward, nor concave

- Tip of nose should be slightly higher than the muzzle

- Nose is broad and black

Expression

- Must be alert and intelligent

Eyes

- Dark brown

- Placed frontally

- Generous

- Not too small, or protruding or too deep set

- Preferably, eyelids display pigmented rims

The wrinkling of the forehead combined with their mood-mirroring character gives the Boxer canine its unique expressive quality.

Proportion, Size and Substance

Proportion

Body profile should be square so that a horizontal line beginning at the front of the forechest to the rear of the upper thigh is equal to the length of a vertical line from the tip of the withers to the ground.

Size

- Adult females: 21 1/2 to 23 1/2 inches at the withers

- Adult males: 23 - 25 inches at the withers

- Correct quality and balance in the individual is of primary importance because there is no size disqualification.

Substance

- Individual displays balanced musculature and is sturdy. Larger bones should be prevalent in males than females.

Ears

- Set at the highest points on the temples of the skull

- Ears must be customarily cropped, long, tapering and raised when the canine is alert

- Un - cropped ears must be of moderate measurements, lying flat, thin and close to the cheeks when rested; falling forward with distinguishing creases when alert

Jaw Structure and Bite

- Bite is undershot

- Lower jaw should protrude past the upper and slightly curve upward

- Lower jaw incisor teeth should display straight with the canines
  preferably up front following the same line to give the jaw the greatest width possible

- Upper line of the incisors is convex slightly; the corner upper incisors must fit snugly at the back of the lower canine teeth on each side

- Teeth and tongue do not stick out when mouth is closed

- Upper jaw is broad, maintains breadth, with a very slight tapering to the front

- Lips are to meet evenly at the front

- Upper lip should be thick and padded, eliminating the frontal space made by the projection of the lower jaw; is laterally supported by the canines of the lower jaw

- Canines must stand far apart and be of good length so that the front surface of the muzzle is broad and 'square-ish'

- Viewed from the side, teeth should show moderate layback

- Chin must be perceptible from both sides as well as front

- An over-lip that obscures the chin is to be penalized

Neck, Topline and Body

Neck

- Round

- Ample length

- Muscular and clean

- No excessive hanging skin (dewlap)

- It should be distinctly arched

- Elegant nape is to blend smoothly into the withers

Back and Topline

- The individuals back is short, muscular, straight, firm, and smooth

- Topline should slightly slope when the Boxer is at attention, and leveled out when in motion

- Chest displays fair width

- The fore chest must be well-defined and visible from the side

- Brisket must be deep and reaches down to the Boxers elbows

- Depth of body at lowest point of the brisket must equal half
the height of the dog at the withers

- Extended ribs far to the rear, well-arched but not barrel-shaped

- Short and muscular loins

- Lower stomach line must be slightly tucked up, and should blend into a graceful curve to the rear

- Croup is to be slightly sloped, flat and broad

- Pelvis should be long; and females must display a broad pelvis

- Tail is set high, docked, and is carried upward

- An undocked tail must be penalized severely

Forequarters

- Shoulders should be long and sloping, it must be close-lying, and not covered excessively with muscle

- Upper arm must be long, and a right angle to the shoulder blade

- Elbows must not press too close to the chest wall or visibly stand out

- Long forelegs, firmly muscled and straight

- When viewed from front, legs must stand parallel to each other

- Pastern is to be strong and distinct, slanting slightly, and stands almost perpendicular to the ground

- Dewclaws can be removed

- Feet must be compact, neither turning in nor out, toes are well-arched

Hindquarters

- Hindquarters must be strongly muscled; angulation must be in balance with the forequarters

- Thighs must be broad and curved; its breech musculature hard and developed strongly

- Upper and lower thighs must display long

- Legs must be well-angulated at the stifle; not too steep or over-angulated, "let down" hock joints are clearly defined

- When inspected from behind, hind legs have to be straight, with its hock joints not leaning in or out

- The leg below the hock (metatarsus) must be nearly perpendicular to the ground; a slight slope to the rear is permissible

- Metatarsus has to be short, clean, and strong

- Boxer does not sport rear dewclaws

Gait

- On profile, proper front and rear angulation is displayed in a smooth, efficient, level-backed, ground covering stride showing a powerful drive coming from a freely operating rear

- Front legs must display adequate reach to avoid sidewinding, interference or overlap

- Shoulders should be trim and the elbows must not flare out

- Legs should be parallel until gaiting narrows the track in line with increasing speed; the legs then come under the body but must never cross

- Line from shoulder down the length of the leg must remain straight but not necessarily perpendicular to the ground

- A Boxer's rump should not roll when viewed from the rear

- Hind paws must dig in and track relatively correct with the front

- A Boxer's gait must always appear smooth and powerful, not stilted or inefficient

Docking and Cropping

In some countries the practice of cropping and docking is still done. However in others, standards have changed. As of 2012, it is still common to see show dogs sport the cropped ear appearance in the US and in Canada. This practice, however, is under strong opposition and scrutiny by the American Veterinary Medical Association.

The American Kennel Club changed its standard in March of 2005 including a description of the un-cropped ear version of the canine to be included as well and to penalize severely those who don't sport the docked tail. In the United Kingdom, sort of short-tailed (or bobtailed) canines were naturally developed in anticipation of the banning of docked tails and finally after tireless observation and several periods of controlled breeding, this sort, in 1998, found acceptance in the United Kingdom Kennel Club registry. Presently, the bobtail line is seen in numerous countries worldwide.

The Fédération Cynologique Internationale, or World Canine Organization in Belgium, disqualified the naturally stumpy-tail line in their standards of breeding in 2008. Since then showing of this sort has been banned for showing or exhibition in member countries.

Colors and Coat

The Boxer sports a smooth, shiny coat. Its fur is short and clings close to its skin. Many are fawn or brindle in color and may frequently sport a white belly and/or may have white-socks paws. Flash is how these white markings are referred to and these may go all the way up to its neck or even its face. Those with these markings are typically referred to as "flashy". Denoting a range of tones, fawns can be best described as varied hues from yellow to light tan, mahogany, stag/deer red, and a dark honey-blonde. Red is a moniker many fawn hued guardians describe the color of the coat of their ward in the UK and Europe.

Bridle is a Boxer with black stripes on a background of fawn. There are Boxers whose body is so heavily stripped that it makes their coat appear to be of "reverse bridling". But this is a misnomer as there are still those with fawn coats that sport black stripes. Breeding Standards call for the fawn background to predominate and show through or contrast the bridling.

Black or White - Or Is It?

Purebred black Boxers do not exist since the Boxer does not carry the gene to produce a solid black coat.

As for what is conventionally called a "white" Boxer, it may neither be called rare or albinos since about 20-25% of all Boxers are born white. These white - colored coat sorts are also, in fact, either brindle or fawn with an excessive amount of white markings on its body which overlays its base coat. Just the same with fair-skinned humans, light-coated Boxers are much more prone to sunburns and skin cancers commonly seen in this fair-colored canine sort. The gene responsible for the Boxers white marks, called the piebald gene, is also said to be the cause of deafness in Boxers. It is estimated that about 18% of white Boxers suffer from partial or total deafness in one or both ears. However, this number is contested by rescue organizations claiming this may be an underestimation of numbers.

Breeders used to euthanize white pups at birth because of the possibility of deafness. It was deemed unethical to breed or sell dogs which may later display a deformity of some sort, hence the reason for euthanizing white pups. However, present breeders are much more reluctant to euthanize and presently is able to give these white-coated pups a chance of life through neutering and placing them in pet homes where they may instead stand to thrive and be taken in and cared for later.

Temperament

The Boxer is a playful breed who makes for an active, energetic companion. Its loyalty takes shape as you both get to know each other better. It is bright, funny and has a pleasant manner when dealing with little children. They are spirited and playful but also very protective of their young humans which make them instant hits with families. They are strong dogs who are active and require a good amount of exercise to stave off licking, chewing or digging also called boredom-associated behaviors. Inappropriate obedience training may be the culprit for the Boxer earning a reputation of being a "headstrong" canine.

Their working breed traits and smarts have shown time and again that corrections-based training is useless to their sort. Like other animals, Boxers show better response to techniques of positive reinforcement, like training with a clicker (clicker training). This approach is based on behaviorism and operant conditioning, offering the canine and opportunity to problem-solve on its own and think independently.

It is by nature not a vicious or aggressive breed. Once attached to a family it builds a strong sense of responsibility toward its guardians and displays visible protection to them.

Dogs of all breeds, sorts and kinds share one thing in common and that is the need to socialize with humans and other dogs. Not only are Boxers friendly to two-legged humans - Boxers extends great patience and affection with puppies and smaller canines too.

They may display an amount of anxiety and may find it difficult to be around other dogs at the onset of a meeting. The same is to be said for canines of the same gender and the larger sort. However with proper integration and supervision during socialization Boxers find comfort in human or canine companionship.

Chapter Eight: Breeding Your Boxer Dogs

Are you prepared in breeding your Boxer dog? One must be fully prepared before breeding. Breeding involves many veterinarian bills, it's important for you to have a financial capability. Newborn puppies also need to a lot of attention and caring. Breeding will challenge your physical, emotional and financial aspect!

Even the best breeders experience loss. Read on if you really want to become a breeder but take note that there are a lot of things that you should know. This chapter will give you an idea of breeding one.

Basic Dog Breeding Information

The first rule that to you have to understand and follow is that breeding is best left to professional breeders. But of course, it is also essential that you know the basics of breeding a dog. A lot of things are involved, and it is important that you know your responsibilities and all the things that you need to observe to ensure that the breeding will produce healthy Boxer puppies.

There is somewhat a high level of loss in puppies. This is caused by different kinds of reasons, and can also happen in any breed not only on Boxer dogs, but this happens more often in toy breeds. Anyone who is breeding must understand and accept that puppies may die inexplicably at times. It is heartbreaking and tragic of course.

When Dogs Mate

When a female dog or what they termed it as the 'bitch' is in heat, there are a few signs that can point towards her beginning this process. Below are the following signs you will notice:

- Being nervous
- Easily spooked

- Easily distracted
- Urinating more than usual

Her personality may also alter due to the abrupt change in her hormones. Male dogs are ready to breed from the age of 18 months to 4/5 years old according to breeding dogs Info center. An interesting fact about male dogs is that when they hit the age around 10 years old, the semen they produce will not be capable of impregnating a female.

Female Dog Ovulation

A lot of breeders today use lab tests to measure Progesterone, vaginal cytology, and luteinizing hormone to determine when ovulation occurs. Breeders know that the cycle is usually 21 days despite what some male dogs think. What may be normal for one dog may differ from another. Some bitches' cycle on schedule, while others mate and ovulate from 12-21 days. Some have 'clear heats', false or flaky seasons, or even false pregnancies.
On the next page are the average estrus changes an owner may expect in normal heat cycles.

- **Day 1:** Attention to rear and licking. Discharge is bright or dark red color, swelling of the vulva. You can start counting heat cycle from when the blood hits the ground.

- **Day 2 – 7:** Bright red discharge with swelling increases

- **Day 8 – 10:** The color begins to lighten and turn into pinkish. Swelling is at peak and the vulva has a spongy feel and look.

- **Day 9 – 14:** The color changes from light pink to clear or straw colored. The swelling is down and the vulva may appear hard or dry on edges.

- **Day 14 – 21:** Color clears, discharge and swelling is almost gone and bitch may already act receptive, but is still snappy. You can count 58-62 days for puppies! But there also exceptions to the rule. Some bitched may mate and conceive as late as 22 days.

Tips for Breeding Your Boxer Dogs

Now that you know the basics about breeding dogs you can learn the specifics about Boxer breed. The Boxer dog has a gestation period lasting about 50 - 60 days (2 – 3 months).

The gestation period is the period of time following conception during which the puppies develop in the mother's uterus. The average litter size for the Boxer breed is between 3 to 10 puppies. The highest recorded newborn puppies for Boxer dogs are 15 puppies!

To increase your chances of a successful breeding, you need to keep track of your Boxer dog's estrus cycle. Once your female reaches the point of ovulation, you can introduce her to the male dog and let nature take its course. Breeding behavior varies slightly from one breed to another, but you can expect the male dog to mount the female from behind (as long as she is receptive). If the breeding is successful, conception will occur and the gestation period will begin.

While the puppies are developing inside your female boxer's uterus, you need to take special care to make sure the female is properly nourished. You do not need to make changes to your dog's diet until the fourth or fifth week of pregnancy. At that point you should slightly increase her daily rations in an amount proportionate to her weight gain. It is generally best to offer your dog free feeding because she will know how much she needs to eat. Make sure your dog's diet is high in protein as well as calories and fat to support the development of her puppies – calcium is also very important.

Labor Process of Boxer Dogs

By around the seventh or eighth week of pregnancy you should start preparing yourself and your dog for the whelping. This is the time when you should set up a whelping box where your female dog can comfortably give birth to her puppies. Place the box in a quiet, dim area and line it with newspapers and old towels for comfort. The closer it gets to the whelping, the more time your dog will spend in the whelping box, preparing it for her litter.

During the last week of your Boxer's pregnancy you should start taking her internal temperature at least once per day – this is the greatest indicator of impending labor. The normal body temperature for a dog is about 100°F to 102°F (37.7°C to 38.8°C). When your dog's body temperature drops, you can expect contractions to begin within 24 hours or so. Prior to labor, your dog's body temperature may drop as low as 98°F (36.6°C) – if it gets any lower, contact your veterinarian.

Once your Boxer starts going into labor, you can expect her to show some obvious signs of discomfort. Your dog might start pacing restlessly, panting, and switching positions. The early stages of labor can often last for several hours and contractions may occur as often as 10 minutes apart. If your Boxer dog has contractions for more than 2 hours without any of the puppies being born, contact your veterinarian immediately! Once your dog starts giving birth, the puppies will arrive about every ten to thirty minutes following thirty minutes of straining.

After each puppy is born, they will lick the puppy clean; it may even eat the umbilical cord because it is animal instinct. This also helps to stimulate the puppy to start breathing on his own. Once all of the puppies have been born, the mother will expel the rest of the placenta (the afterbirth) and then let the puppies start nursing. It is essential that the puppies begin nursing within one hour of being born because this is when they will receive the colostrum from the mother. Colostrum is the first milk produced and it contains a variety of nutrients as well as antibodies to protect the pups until their own immune systems have time to develop. In addition to making sure that the puppies are feeding, you should also make sure that the mother eats soon after whelping.

Like other puppies, Boxer pups are small in size; some of these puppies are also born blind, with their eyes and ears closed, so they are completely dependent on the mother for several weeks. Around 3rd week, the puppies will open their eyes and their ears will become erect sometime after. As the puppies grow, they will start to become increasingly active and the will grow very quickly as long as they are properly fed by the mother.

At six weeks of age is the time you should begin weaning the puppies by offering them small amounts of puppy food soaked in water or broth. The puppies might sample small bits of solid food even while they are still nursing and the mother will general wean the puppies by around the eight week, with or without your help. If you plan to sell the puppies, be sure not to send them home unless they are fully weaned at least eight weeks old. You should also take steps to start socializing the puppies from an early age to make sure they turn into well-adjusted adults.

Chapter Nine: Avoid Health Issues

Reputable breeders would attest that the Boxer is possibly one of the most popular dogs of any given period in time. They are fiercely loyal and extremely loving of their humans.

The Boxer is one breed that continues to enjoy popularity the world over. Many people seek out Boxers to take in for security, aide, companionship and love.

In this next chapter you will read about some of the conditions a Boxer may be more susceptible to than others.

We encourage you to ask your vet about other health concerns you may have questions about.

Health

It is imperative that future and possible caregivers know what they are getting into when they take in a Boxer as an addition to their home. Like other breeds, the Boxer is prone to some conditions that guardians and caregivers should be aware of to empower themselves to avoid such eventualities.

Here you will find out more about the health of the Boxer, how to take care of it and all you need to know to have your Boxer enjoy a long and healthy life with your family.

Possible Health Conditions to Discuss with Your Vet

Acne

Boxers, like teenagers also suffer from acne as they transition during puberty. Acne may not seem like much of a concern but remember that it could lead to more serious infections if not treated. At the very least it could be cause of scarring.

Aortic Stenosis

This medical condition of the dog's heart could affect most dogs but the Boxer is more prone to it than other breeds. This is also an inherited condition and alarmingly may be passed down to pups. Therefore it is vital that this condition is detected early on in the pups' life. Suffering from severe Aortic Stenosis is a very serious condition. This is often found during a routine examination with a vet and is detected as a heart murmur.

Symptoms

- The Boxer may seem tired and weak

- Appetite falls

- Breathing is labored

- Coughing or panting

- May experience fainting spells after a rigorous activity

- In severe cases, the pulsation in its neck is visibly seen even when asleep or resting.

Aortic Stenosis

A Boxer of either gender with a mild case of Aortic Stenosis can potentially pass this on to the next generation which will cause the pups a short life afflicted by this disease. For this reason, reputable breeders will never breed a dog, whether dam or sire, who has exhibited even the mildest form of this condition.

Boxers being considered for breeding purposes should most certainly be tested for this condition by a canine-cardiologist before pairing (it) up with a mate.

A Boxer can enter a breeding program once it is cleared of the condition and is at least a year old.

Arthritis

This is a very real condition in most domesticated pets, canine or feline. What needs to be kept in mind is that arthritis is not just a condition for mature or aging pets. It is also a condition to look out for in young pups.

Causes

- If the Boxer has an injury to its ligaments it can cause arthritis.

- Obesity can speed up development of arthritis in canines.

- As a dog matures its joints may be genetically weakened and contribute to the condition.

- In Boxer puppies, proper bone development or failure thereof could be the culprit.

Symptoms

- Weakness of limbs.

- Seeming tiredness and fatigue.

- Shows signs of difficulty getting up from lying down, difficulty in motion.

- Swollen joints.

- Pain is communicated by retreating, not socializing and sometimes aggression.

When a canine shows any of these symptoms or if it is known that the dog recently had an injury, a vet should immediately be consulted.

Boxer/Canine Bloat

This Boxer health problem is a very serious one and could lead to fatality if not recognized and treated immediately.

A condition, which can occur at any age, it is also one that can be avoided if the Boxers guardian knows how to take preventative measures.

The Boxer is the 16th most likely to contract Bloat of the 200 dog breeds in existence and it is 3.7 times more likely to develop it than typical mixed breeds.

Canine Bloat, when serious can be fatal up to 50% of cases, is also known as Gastric Dilatation Volvulus. Bloat occurs when the dog's stomach gets distended with fluid and gas and there is a slight rotation of the stomach. Another indicator is that the distended stomach twists anywhere from 180 degrees to a full 360. The spleen rotates out as well because it is connected to the stomach wall. This is the volvulus condition and is life threatening.

Bloat will happen when gastro esophageal junction becomes obstructed and the canine is unable to expel trapped air, food or gases.

Causes

- Eating too fast and overeating are the most common reasons

- Rigorous exercise immediately before or immediately after a meal

- Gulping a large amount of water right after eating

- Stress

Signs

- Drooling

- Pacing

- Stomach feels taut to the touch

- Discomfort

- Head hangs low

- Weakness

Symptoms

- Excessive drooling

- Moaning and whining

- A visibly taut and tight stomach that protrudes and is distended more than that is normal

- The canine may walk abnormally due to pain

- It may display aggressiveness if it is in pain and may retreat from other pets and people

When a Boxer starts displaying these symptoms it is vital to get the canine to the vet.

How to Prevent Boxer/Canine Bloat

This canine health problem can be avoided if you know what to do in order to avoid Canine Bloat. Below are ways to prevent this from happening to a Boxer.

- No exercise or strenuous activity two hours after feeding. Put off walking a Boxer for an hour after a meal.

- Use a stainless steel slow-feeding bowl to encourage slow eating and drinking. Food mustn't be wolfed down and water shouldn't be gulped in large amounts after a meal.

- To avoid gulping large amounts of water always make sure the Boxer is well-hydrated before, during and after walks. Always bring a bottle of water for it to drink periodically when out for a walk.

- Only choose healthy home cooked meals or high quality and trusted brands.

- Greasy, spicy human food is an absolutely great no-no for a Boxer as this may lead to canine bloat. Never overfeed a Boxer and be sure to follow proper feeding guidelines in terms of amount and frequency.

- Slow-feeding and drinking bowls should be placed at floor level as extended observation and studies have shown that raised bowls increase the chances of canine bloat.

A Boxer suffering from Bloat is to be immediately taken to the ER of an animal hospital as this is the only place the canine can receive the proper medical attention. A Boxer under treatment will need to be in hospital for a few days at the least as water and food will be restricted and the canine will have to receive fluids intravenously.

Surgery on a Boxer suffering from canine bloat is a procedure that can be done if emergency procedures do not work. If you are considering a Boxer as an addition to your family be sure to talk to experienced guardians, caregivers, upstanding breeders and veterinarians about canine bloat, its causes, symptoms and treatment.

Over the 20 year study by the University of Georgia which studied 82 dog breeds (at least 100 dogs of each breed), it became apparent that the Boxer is the 5th breed of canines most likely to die of cancer. These could include cancer of the lymph nodes, skin cancer, breast and mammary gland cancer (this can be reduced with early spaying) as well as bone cancer.

Other Boxer conditions that a potential guardian or caregiver should be aware of and talk about with an animal doctor would be Cardiomyopathy (Heart Condition), ear mites, ear infections, eye disease, heartworms, hip dysplasia, disease of the colon, canine back problem, stomach disease, red mange, hypothyroidism, and seizures.

This chapter has hopefully enlightened you, the reader, of the medical conditions that a Boxer is susceptible of getting. This is a reminder to ask about the history of the canine. You want your own Boxer buddy to live a long, healthy and happy life at home and the aim here was to give vital information on how you can better take care of a Boxer should you choose to bring home one to the family.

Boxer Dogs Care Sheet

You have come to the end of this book. By now it is hoped that the information within this book has shed light and has afforded you a closer look at the sweet, lovable Boxer a little more. Now that you've found out what it would take for you as guardian to be a caregiver of a Boxer we pray you have come closer to deciding on taking in your own Boxer pal. We hope this book, which was aimed to enlighten you of what to expect when thinking about bringing in a Boxer to your mix has done just that. Further research on your end is greatly encouraged.

Go ahead and ask experienced guardians, neighborhood vets and registered breeders of upstanding repute more about the Boxer. Networking with other Boxer caregivers and sharing best practices is a precious exchange of which you should make a habit. However, keep in mind that each dog, no matter what pedigree or breed, has its own distinct characteristics, personality, traits and behavior. Each dog will generally display commonality but will still have stand out, unique personalities.

Here is a quick glance, and last once over of important information to keep in mind as we close this chapter and book. Here is hoping that you enjoy many years of playful days, warm, cuddly nights and abounding joy as you bring home your very own loyal, friendly, affectionate and amusingly boisterous Boxer.

A Summary of Facts about the Boxer

Pedigreed: American Kennel Club

Group: Molossus

Breed Size: Medium

Height: up to 25 inches tall for males, females measure in a tad shorter at 23 ½ inches from the ground

Weight: 60 lbs for females and up to 70 lbs. for males

Coat Texture: short, cropped close to skin

Color: Brindle, White, Fawn, Black Mask White Markings, White Markings,

Eyes: expressively dark eyes

Ears: folded ears drooping toward face

Tail: all Boxers originally were born with long tails and ears which stick out. Docking and cropping is done early on in the pups life with time tested procedures that alleviate possible future injury to the dog's tail and ears.

Temperament: it needs lots of your attention and loves being around and interacting with its humans. It gets on well with smaller pets like some cats and most toy dogs as well as larger, mild-tempered canines.

Strangers: weary but nonviolent toward strangers

Other Pets: with the caregivers patient integration it readily adapts to other pets, like smaller dogs, larger dogs with mild traits you may own

Training: Highly trainable and responds well to positive reinforcement

Exercise Needs: frequent, lively exercise is strongly encouraged for Boxers to burn up their stored energy. Frequent supervised forays outside the home are encouraged.

Health Conditions: Boxers like other pets can be prone to some diseases more than others. Please carefully read through Chapter Four to find out a little more about what can be avoided to avert the likelihood of contracting illnesses to which they may be prone.

Lifespan: typical average lifespan is 12 -13 years

Basic Nutritional Information of the Boxer

- Diet must be rich in meats (chicken, veal, turkey, lamb and beef), carbohydrates and some vegetables like broccoli, sweet peas, sweet potatoes, potatoes, carrots, string beans

- Water Consumption - frequent replenishment of fresh water is strongly recommended

- Feeding Amount - varies on specific factors like weight, size and age.

- Feeding Frequency - depends on age and weight

- Make sure that you as guardian set a scheduled time for feeding and never feed it in between meals saves for treats.

Boxer Accessories

- Dog crate

- Pet bed

- Poop scooper, or small plastic pail and shovel

- Blanket

- Carrier/ transportable kennel

- Dog toys and treats

- Slow-feed bowls for food and water

- Brush

- Toothbrush

- Leash

- Collar

- Clippers, guillotine, or rotary stone grinder for nails

Index

C

D

Q

R

S

Photo Credits

Page 1 Photo by winkimedia via Pixabay, https://pixabay.com/en/dog-puppy-pet-young-dog-small-dog-1796040/

Page 10 Photo by fh4life via Pixabay, https://pixabay.com/en/dog-smile-pet-animal-cute-689684/

Page 16 Photo by Myriams-Fotos via Pixabay, https://pixabay.com/en/dog-boxer-pet-black-and-white-play-1144889/

Page 33 Photo by sdnet01 via Pixabay, https://pixabay.com/en/dog-boxer-canine-animal-pet-white-893133/

Page 43 Photo by Alexas_Fotos via Pixabay, https://pixabay.com/en/boxer-dogs-dogs-good-aiderbichl-1321231/

Page 51 Photo by geliguti via Pixabay, https://pixabay.com/en/dog-pet-race-boxer-animal-108678/

References

"1938 Official Boxer Standard" Harvel Boxers
<http://www.harvelboxers.com/1938.html>

"All about the Boxer Dog Cost" Pet Sitter Land
<https://petsittersireland.com/all-about-the-boxer-dog-cost-
pricing-breeders-and-more/>

"Best Food for a Boxer Dog" All Boxer Info
<http://www.allboxerinfo.com/best-food-for-boxer-dog>

"Boxer Dog" Wikipedia
<https://en.wikipedia.org/wiki/Boxer_(dog)>

"Boxer Dogs" Boxer World
<https://boxerworld.com/>

"Boxer Dog Health Problems" All Boxer Info

<http://www.allboxerinfo.com/boxer-dog-health-problems>

"Bleeding Disorder in Dogs" PetMD

<http://www.petmd.com/dog/conditions/cardiovascular/c_d
g_von_willebrand_disease>

"Cataracts in Dogs" PetMD
<http://www.petmd.com/dog/conditions/eye/c_dg_cataract>

"Cost of Owning a Dog" Pet Education
<http://www.peteducation.com/article.cfm?c=2+2106&aid=1543>
 "Crate Training" American Dog Trainers Network

<http://inch.com/~dogs/cratetraining.html>
"Dog Behavior Training – Proven Techniques to Help Solve Problem Behaviors" Dog Training Central

<http://www.dog-obedience-training-review.com/dog-
     behavior-training.html>

"Dog Nutrition Tips." ASPCA

 <http://www.aspca.org/pet-care/dog-care/dog-nutrition-
  tips>

 "Estrus Cycle in Dogs" VCA

<http://www.vcahospitals.com/main/pet-health-
information/article/animal-health/estrus-cycles-in-
dogs/5778>

 "Getting Started Showing Your Dog" AKC

<http://www.akc.org/events/conformation-dog-
     shows/getting-started-showing/>

"Glaucoma in Dogs" PetMD

<http://www.petmd.com/dog/conditions/eyes/c_dg_glauco
     ma>

"Glossary" Boxerlife.com
<http://boxerlife.com/glossary.html>

"Housebreaking (Potty Training) for Puppies and Adult Dogs." Michele Welton. <http://www.yourpurebredpuppy.com/training/articles/dog-housebreaking.html>

"How to Choose a Good Puppy (Picking the Best Puppy in a Litter)" Michele Welton <http://www.yourpurebredpuppy.com/buying/articles/how-to-choose-a-puppy.html>

"How to Choose an Experienced Dog Breeder" PetMD

<http://www.petmd.com/dog/care/evr_dg_breeders>

"How to Choose High-Quality Dog Food" Alphadog

<https://alphadogfood.com/choose-high-quality-dog-food>

"How to Find a Responsible Dog Breeder" The Humane Society of the United States

<http://www.humanesociety.org/issues/puppy_mills/tips/finding_responsible_dog_breeder.html?referrer=https://www.google.com/>

"How to introduce a new puppy to older Boxer"
Boxer World

<https://boxerworld.com/forums/threads/how-to-introduce-a-new-puppy-to-older-boxer.138870/>

"Inflammatory Skin Disease in Dogs" PetMD
<http://www.petmd.com/dog/conditions/skin/c_dg_sebaceous_adenitis>

"Intervertebral Disk Disease (IVDD)" ExpertVet
<http://www.expertvet.com/articles/intervertebral-disk-disease-ivdd>

"Keeping Your Puppy Safe at Home" Erin Ollila
<http://www.hillspet.com/en/us/dog-care/new-pet-parent/puppy-proofing-your-home>

"New to Dog Showing?" The Kennel Club
<http://www.thekennelclub.org.uk/activities/dog-showing/new-to-dog-showing/>

"Owning a Dog Cost" Costhelper
<http://pets.costhelper.com/owning-dog.html>

"Preparing for a dog show" Your Dog
<http://www.yourdog.co.uk/Dog-Activities/preparing-for-a-dog-show.html>

"Puppy proofing basics" Wendy Wilson
<https://www.cesarsway.com/dog-care/puppies/puppy-proofing-basics>

"Responsible Breeding" AKC

<http://www.akc.org/dog-breeders/responsible-breeding/>

"Routine Vaccinations for Puppies and Dogs" WebMD

<http://pets.webmd.com/dogs/guide/routine-vaccinations-puppies-dogs>

"Sleeping Arrangement for New Puppy" BFF Dog Training LLC

<http://www.bfftraining.com/available-puppies/puppy-behavior-problems/sleeping-arrangement-for-new-puppy/>

"Socializing Your Puppy or Adult Dog to Get Along With the World" Michele Welton
<http://www.yourpurebredpuppy.com/training/articles/dog-socializing.html>

"Ten Tips for Showing Your Dog" Kelly Roper
<http://dogs.lovetoknow.com/dog-information/ten-tips-showing-your-dog>

"Thinking of Buying a Puppy? Find a Responsible Breeder" AKC

<http://www.akc.org/press-center/facts-stats/responsible-breeders/>

"Tips for Choosing a Healthy Puppy" Susan Koranki
<http://www.fidosavvy.com/choosing-a-healthy-puppy.html>

"Understanding Bloat and Torsion" Kifka Borzoi
<http://www.kifka.com/Elektrik/Bloat.htm>

"Vaccinations for Your Pet" ASPCA

<http://www.aspca.org/pet-care/general-pet-
care/vaccinations-your-pet>

"Vaccination Schedule for Dogs and Puppies" Pet Education

<http://www.peteducation.com/article.cfm?c=2+2115&aid=95
0>

"Vaccinating Your Pet" RSPCA

<https://www.rspca.org.uk/adviceandwelfare/pets/general/v
accinating>

"Want to Do Well at the Dog Show? Prepare All You Can
Ahead of Time" AKC

<http://www.akc.org/content/dog-training/articles/prepare-
ahead-of-time/>

"Weaning Puppies" Race Foster, DVM.
<http://www.peteducation.com/article.cfm?c=2+1651&aid=88
7>

"Weaning Puppies from their Mother" PetMD

<http://www.petmd.com/dog/puppycenter/nutrition/evr_dg
_weaning_puppies_from_their_mother#>

"Weaning Puppies: What to Do" WebMD

<http://pets.webmd.com/dogs/weaning-puppies-what-do>

"Where Should My Puppy Sleep?" Dog Life Training

<http://doglifetraining.com/2012/08/where-should-my-puppy-sleep/>

Feeding Baby
Cynthia Cherry
978-1941070000

Axolotl
Lolly Brown
978-0989658430

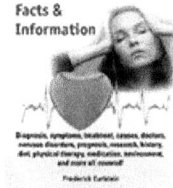

Dysautonomia, POTS
Syndrome
Frederick Earlstein
978-0989658485

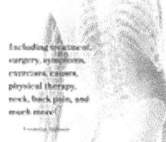

Degenerative Disc
Disease Explained
Frederick Earlstein
978-0989658485

Sinusitis, Hay Fever,
Allergic Rhinitis Explained
Frederick Earlstein
978-1941070024

Wicca
Riley Star
978-1941070130

Zombie Apocalypse
Rex Cutty
978-1941070154

Capybara
Lolly Brown
978-1941070062

Eels As Pets
Lolly Brown
978-1941070167

Scabies and Lice Explained
Frederick Earlstein
978-1941070017

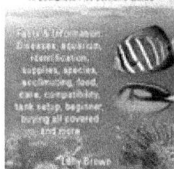

Saltwater Fish As Pets
Lolly Brown
978-0989658461

Torticollis Explained
Frederick Earlstein
978-1941070055

Kennel Cough
Lolly Brown
978-0989658409

Physiotherapist, Physical
Therapist
Christopher Wright
978-0989658492

Rats, Mice, and Dormice
As Pets
Lolly Brown
978-1941070079

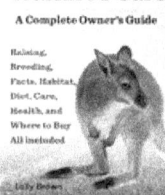

Wallaby and Wallaroo Care
Lolly Brown
978-1941070031

Bodybuilding Supplements
Explained
Jon Shelton
978-1941070239

Demonology
Riley Star
978-19401070314

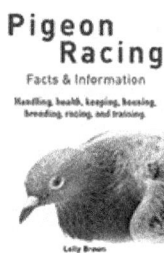

Pigeon Racing
Lolly Brown
978-1941070307

Dwarf Hamster
Lolly Brown
978-1941070390

Cryptozoology
Rex Cutty
978-1941070406

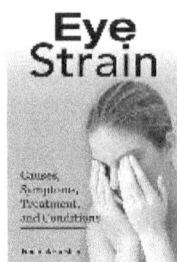

Eye Strain
Frederick Earlstein
978-1941070369

Inez The Miniature Elephant
Asher Ray
978-1941070353

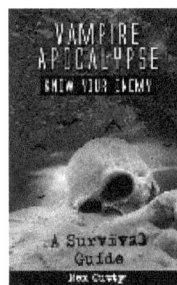

Vampire Apocalypse
Rex Cutty
978-1941070321

www.ingramcontent.com/pod-product-compliance
Lightning Source LLC
LaVergne TN
LVHW051642080426
835511LV00016B/2442